CHRONICALLY BEAUTIFUL

II

Written By

Camille Soleil

Copyright © 2024

Dedication

My series of books of poetry, "Chronically Beautiful" are for everyone living with a chronic condition and everyone helping those people; As well as my Mom, my Dad, my therapist, my caregivers and the NF community. Give yourself grace. You are so strong.

Acknowledgment

In honor of My Papa, James Thoms,

Table of Contents

Sometimes

Sometimes I don't want to talk about it,
sometimes I do.
sometimes I want to talk about it,
but not with you.

Sometimes, my head screams,
I just want to yell into the void,
When things get all foggy and dizzied and, I can't do the things I've
enjoyed.

No, sometimes it's better not to tell you,
Because I tell you too much,
I worry you'll think I'm always suffering when I'm not.

Though I want someone to see
What it's like being me,
When I'm broken, weak, and down.
I'm not always the positive person
That I've built my façade around

I cry real tears, I spit fire from my tongue.
Yelling at something that I can't see or someone.

No, I'm not mad at anyone
My only grievance is this:
Why do I have to struggle with this thing I can't fix?

I can pop pills for days.
I can have my body sliced into.
I can distract myself from seeing what I don't want to see...

Though then comes the weight that rests heavy on my shoulders.
I have to look you in the eye,
And address you and smolder

You have no right,
To make my life not seem like mine,
make me hide my pain from the world,
And pretend that I am fine.
Sometimes, you're too heavy to carry,
And I look for some help...
Without feeling like a burden or a victim for asking.

The cruel fate is that this will never end
My relationship with you...
But I'll be dammed
If you take away love,
Which is my biggest defense against you.
And you won't
I won't let you.

So my friends, my loves, I want you to know...
Sometimes, I don't want to talk about it.
Sometimes I do.
Sometimes, I want to talk about it, just not with you.
Though that does not mean that I don't love you.

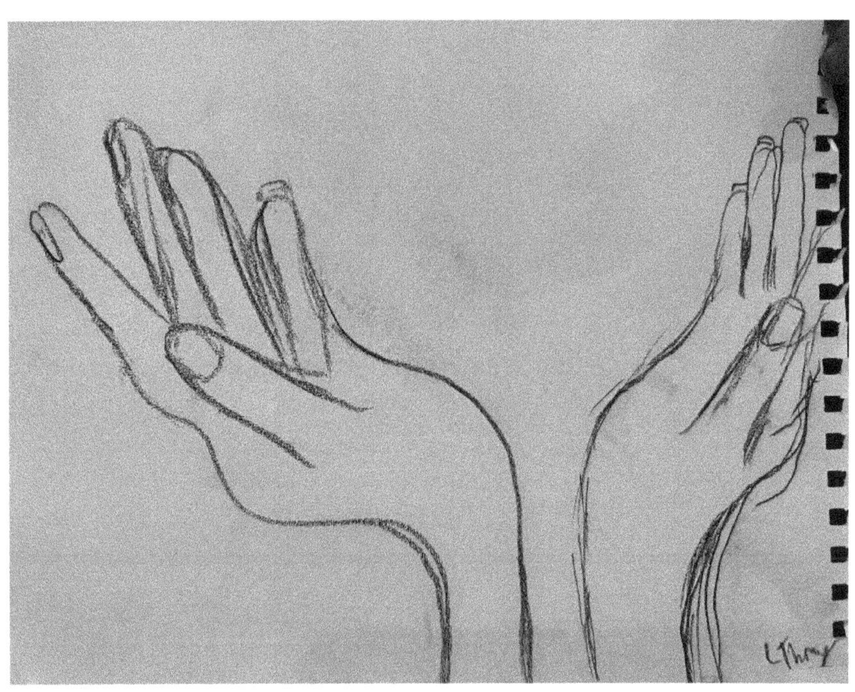

Camille Soleil

Feelings

Patience little girl, do not fret over the unknown
You are safe here and now
no need to feel alone.

The sensations they aren't pleasant
You want to run and flee.
Instead, although uncomfortable, you can let them be.

"No," I say, "I can't do that, these feelings just aren't right."
"No, they're not, but stressing will keep them in too tight"

"So what do I do? Just sit in my own suffering? Try not to push them away?"
"Welcome them, say hi, they may not choose to stay."

"This is hard. I do not know what lies behind each day."
"We never do. So much is life. We're in a constant sway."

"Each day brings new and dries out the old, isn't that amazing?
"So do not fret; each day will be better and feel as good as an old sweater."

Spring

The world is filled of stars and gifts.

We are magnetic,

And cling to each other as it shifts.

How astonishing it is,

To see its beauty with you.

The pollen falling from the trees.

The life repeating new.

The flowers, they hold secrets.

The soft beauty on earth.

Their petals riding on the wind,

Spreading seeds to be unearthed.

The seeds will wait till your life need refreshment,

Until they show their face.

For in one single flower, there holds so much never-ending grace.

Camille Soleil

NF2

I saw the signs you tried to give

And I dismissed them as I pushed to just live

I thought I could outrun you

I thought you wouldn't last

I scraped for the surface while you pulled at my feet

I wanted you to stay away as I politely asked

Haven't I been through enough?

Don't drag me down again.

I know that's where you like me

But I'm trying to find Zen

I'm making peace with what I can't change

And that's really hard

But I will not go easy

When you try to put me behind bars

I actually do have a say in what you do

For only I can see through you

I won't submit

Say, "Well, what can I do?

It's just my disease of NF2."

Many people say that's what I should do

But I was born a fighter

Though, at times, I want to put my arms down

Take off the gloves

Get out of the ring

Though that wouldn't do a damn thing

Then nothing would get done

You'd pull me apart

But if we're together, we can seem to make our pain into art.

smile

Camille Soleil

The Little

Raindrops seen through sunroofs.

The way milk swirls when added to tea.

Bubbles blowing through the dish soap bottle while washing the dishes.

We don't always notice the beauties, but they're there.

It just depends on if we're able to see them.

If our brains are stressed, all around us, then the brain will show us more wrong,

We will see the red without knowing.

"It's raining, everyone on the road will be driving recklessly.

I'm going to get wet, and my hair will fall flat.

I'll have to wear this, and I'll have to change that.

Ugh, I don't want to go out in the rain,

I just want to stay home because I'm in pain.

So many things have to be done before leaving the house

I'll have to bring snacks and my pills and rush out like a mouse.

The doctor's office will be busy, it always is when it rains

Everyone's stupid, and no one has any brains!"

Though then, you can switch when you're too overwhelmed.

Instead of seeing the bad, wipe the slate clean, breathe in and exhale.

This day is how it is,

The rain won't change.

You can be mad and say everything sucks,

then look at the little and find oh so much...

You've hit the brain's limit,

It can't take any more stress.

Look at the little and bring it some rest.

Look through the sunroof while on hold with your doctor.

Listen to the raindrops, to the lightning and thunder.

Look up at the tree you're parked under...

If you weren't on hold, you couldn't do this:

You couldn't laugh at the silly hold song or share in the rains sweet bliss.

When you step out of the car, the cold air refreshes your tired lungs and makes them like new.

Yet all of this we could very well see through...

Though even in pain, the little makes do.

The little is hearing your college friends voice,

It's dancing through rain because that's the more fun choice.

The little is hearing "I see you" when your sad

And slipping too many curse words when you're a little too mad.

There's so much beauty in the little

For big is too much.

Look for the little

It'll keep you in touch

Narrow your scope

You don't have to run the world

Look for the little

Even if it's cold.

The
Pink
Drink
The Pink Drink

The Night

I have these moments at night time when no one's around.

My body is happy,

I feel free from my bound.

I do things I never could attempt in the day,

I dance, and I sing,

Sometimes, even move and get around.

I get into my wheelchair,

And explore my quiet house

The whole place is mine, and the air tastes sweet with no expectations

In the hours between 8 pm and morning

I have no responsibilities, nothing to manage

It's often my favorite time of day

My soul can rest

It can be me

Not sick me

Not boss me

Not mean me

Not angry me

The me that is young

The me that isn't stuck

The me who makes silly videos and doesn't give a fuck

The me that is strawberries and cream

The me that's excited

*This me visits throughout the day, but at night is often when she is
ignited*

She knows she's alone

And though I know in this life I'll need help

She takes every single ounce of the quiet calm and goes wild

Eventually, I'll get tired

And I'll fall asleep

Then, all my routines and stress will likely repeat

Nothing to do between 8 pm and morning

Except to just be me

and I'm so grateful when, in most of these nights, life just lets me be

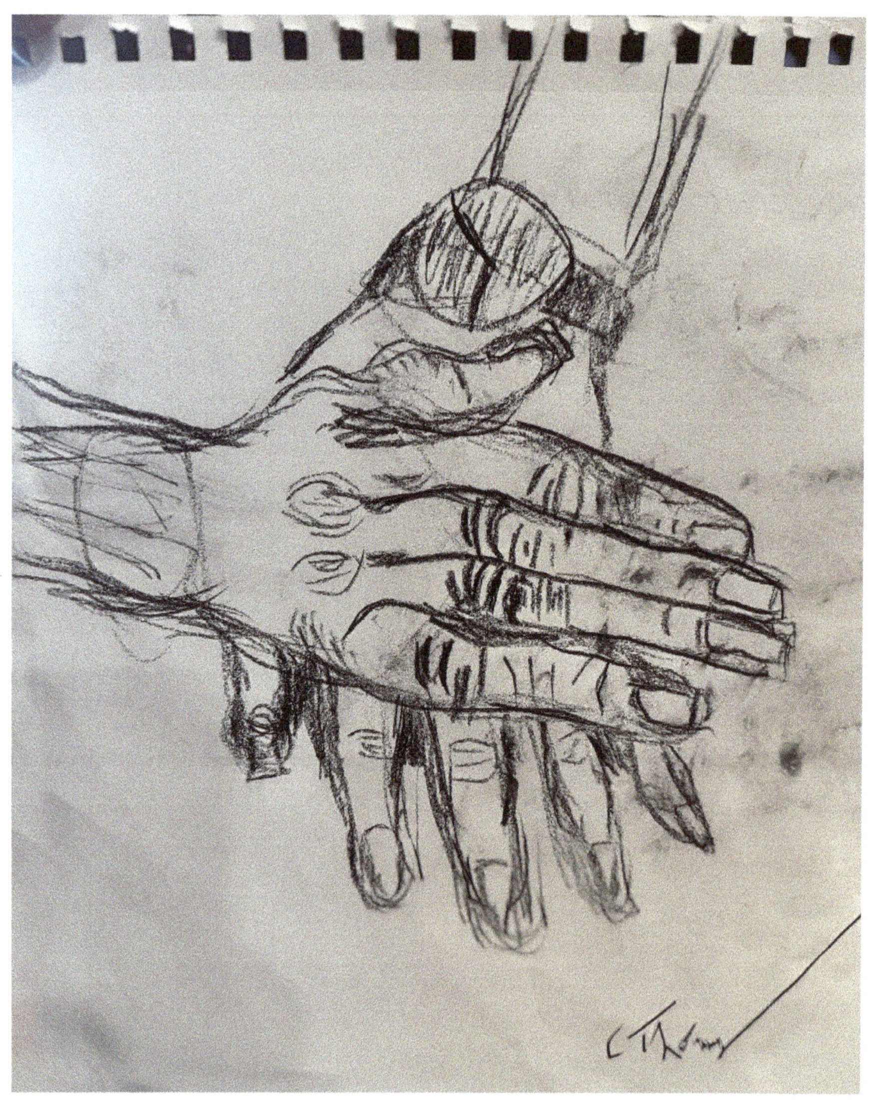

Camille Soleil

Boston

I flew to you to save my life

I trust you with my soul

Even if you also harbor anxieties I can't always control

You're my lifeline and make me sad

I'm clay in your hands

Ready to poke, prod, mold and shape

The only thing you can't do is scrap me and remake

You can be a toxic ex boyfriend

Or the rainbow after the storm

You hold me in your hands

See me as one, and whole

Not broken like in other places

Pounding me down into sand.

Thank you for giving me a safer haven in which I can land

Boston 2

Every time I see you I need to brace myself

Because you'll show me all the trauma I keep inside myself

You'll lay them out one by one

For some there is not much to be done

You'll show me things I don't wish to see

But I need to because they are in Me

The tumors

The cysts

The many unique turns and twists

That make me, me

In my mind that's how I view Boston now

A medical place

A beautiful actuality

Boston 3

You've made my cry and wonder if it will ever end

You've made me vulnerable doing tests and giving results I need time to comprehend

This city has turned dark

It's ripped out some soul

But I took some back

I needed to feel in control

So, I've done crazy things

That this city will keep secret

So every time I see you

I can smile and Remind you to keep it

You've made my cry and wonder if it will ever end

Florence

The one time I blacked-out from alcohol

It was from a night holding pennies in my shoe

Started by spinning on a carousel

It ended by being carried home askew

Sparklers and sticky floors

Spilled drinks, the clubs roar

Drinking beers and other things

Rum and cokes galore

Crooked feet down cobble streets

Laughter drowning our pain

Place to sleep was 3 flights up

Not a care was had

Somehow I wound up back in bed

I forgot exactly how

There's a place on the road where we spilled our drinks

Staining Florence forever now

I Don't Want to Write a Poem

I don't want to write a poem

They always come out sad

They come through best when I am upset, weak, and mad

I don't want to write a poem

Sometimes I'd like not to be me

Because my body and mind do things that cause me to disagree....

Why my hands turn cold

Why I can't catch my breath ?

Why I can't just be normal ?

Why in terms of panic attacks this week I'm on my ..... twentieth ?

I know I have a hard life

But I can't seem to give myself any slack

We go through these appointments then never get any happiness back?

When I'm not at an appointment though

I'm in my own head

Spiraling down tripping over all the things I dread

"Just stop"

"Calm down"

"You're ok"

They say

It doesn't matter how much I believe these words anxiety still never goes away....

Can't you see that's all I want ?!

For this beast to finally go

But my soul and body disagree

Camille Soleil

So on we go with the "crazy" show

I've done the techniques

I've gone on the medicine

But this disease still gives me no peace!

After trauma my body goes through

My mind then demands once I'm home it needs to take a piece of me too

No we can't simply do the thing

We must gear up in fear prior, shake during, and break after

How silly of me to think that after these visits you could just let go.....

but you have lived this routine for most of your life

Though now the soul is calling bullshit

So there's a war going on inside of yourself

Because our soul knows there's beauty and that we deserve it

I feel like a third party living in my skin

Watching these two fight

They'll drag me through mud, won't let me rest, unless we can all unite

So for now my only defense

While watching the fight

Is to spit out my anger through poems

Beauty shown through the writing which pleases my soul

Though it's an anxiety coping skill....

So I guess they agree on this one view....

I don't want to write a poem

I. Need. To.

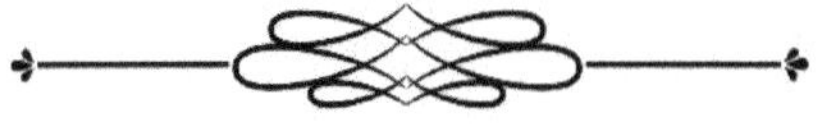

Mothers Advice

"Don't wish for someone else's life"

That's what my mother said to me

You might think their grass is greener

But what you see isn't all it would be

Each trees roots dive deep under the surface

Each life does the same

What you see might look beautiful

When it's really not as easy as they claim

"If everyone put their problems in a bin, you would take your own back"

Everyone's eyes are glued to one another's yet here is the simple fact:

Only you know how to do this

Your roots are in the ground

It'd be harder to dig that out

And face a different sound

You are the queen of this life

As hard as it may be

But you can scream and you can shout

And you'll be heard you see

You've gotten pretty good as this

You have more power then you think

As routine as your life may seem

You're the only one to slay the beast

So when you see someone else's life

Camille Soleil

All shiny and laid back

Remember that you are the queen

And you run your own soundtrack

Mom

I can't tell you everything all the time, I'd be too much.

Only I can truly handle all my stuff.

You speak of pregnancy and childbirth and the pain you suffered, though it ended with the birth of me.

The birth of a life.

That's a great reward for your 9-month sacrifice.

The changes, hormones, never ending pains, they all quieted when I came.

You went through so much hurt to ensure my birth.

Though I know that hurt never fully left.

Every-time I cry.

Every-time I ask why?

And you can't help....

You listen and you comfort, we share in painfully silent moments.

I'm hurting you.

I don't mean to.

I'm letting my silent ailments be seen.

Your hard work should be over.

Though I know it never will.

And for that I feel is on me.

I know though, that it's not.

I can't help but be human.

I just hate to see pain in the woman who gave me this life.

When you share your pains you come along side me,

We share in the hurt.

It's nice when I see past the guarded gates... because I feel like I'm pregnant with no baby at the end.

For me that baby is just me.

When we laugh at filters or your influencers' new trends that's when I feel love.

The same love that you felt when I kicked from inside you.

I need those same loving kicks from the outside, reminding me of my goal.

We're both making me into all I can be....even if it hurts.

Camille Soleil

Dad

You'd harness the moon for me if you could

You're going through something no dad ever should

You're waiting on the day I say I feel good

You'll carry me on your back all over this world

I'm your little girl

And I so desperately want to fulfill your wish

For it's mine as well

Though it's a long journey and time will tell

I hate that this illness is taking me from you

You're my daddy

We used to hold pinkies and eat fondue

When I watch hockey I feel you there

Our hockey bond is something we share

The announcers sound sweet as the noise fills my air

For its my childhood and the noise is

Such a sweet affair

I live only 20 minutes away

Though I'd rather stay in mine

So I can ease my body

But if my soul could speak its mind...

I love you as much as no words could define

*"It's better to beg for forgiveness than ask for permission" and that it
how I live my life*

I love you two times and that means twice

Love

Camille

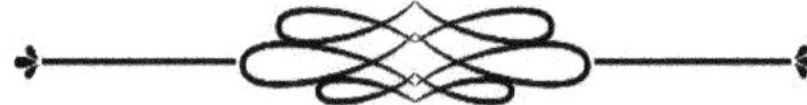

I am strong
and capable

Life

I'm laying on my bed with my puppies at my feet

I'm thinking it's such a shame my past and current self can not meet

She'd tell you about all the fun she's having in college

The high she felt from jumping out of that plane,

She would take my hand and we would walk down memory lane

We'd scroll through glass cases displaying all my past devices

Poles to canes to walkers

Then we'd skip to the past vices

We run past that part I don't need to see

I'm running I say to her with the most amazing glee!

She lets go of my hand and starts to look sad

You can't run anymore?

And she looks at my left hand..

I guess the gigs up she knows the truth

But she wipes the tear falling from my eye

And says "we're still in our youth"

We run up the stairs of my old college apartment

We go into my dorm and find my secret compartment

She opens up my life journal and reads from each page

Suddenly I'm within each memory so realistic it's hard to gauge

Camille Soleil

The best day of my life I had written on paper
Not wanting to let go of that excitement
So I saved it in lead
Friends to boys and boys to scandals
Then she flipped the page
And lit some candles

The familiar crackle from my old wicker scents
Watching it snow and smelling the heat through the vents
"Remember when you would sit here for hours
We had just come from our favorite job
And we would sit in the silence of the snow showers"
My body fills with warmth
As I look out my college window.

"Yes I do" I respond
I miss that window
For lately it's been getting misted over
"That's why I love windows" I tell her
It shows you life even when it feels hard to live
She says "well I thought it was just a window"
"No we didn't realize what it gives."

She holds out her hand
And I grab it tight
She leans to my ear and says

"Everything will be alright"

"You smile at the snow, and dance in the rain, you run home from the bar with one shoe and you also handle all this pain so

"Breathe love…

For right now we're just the same."

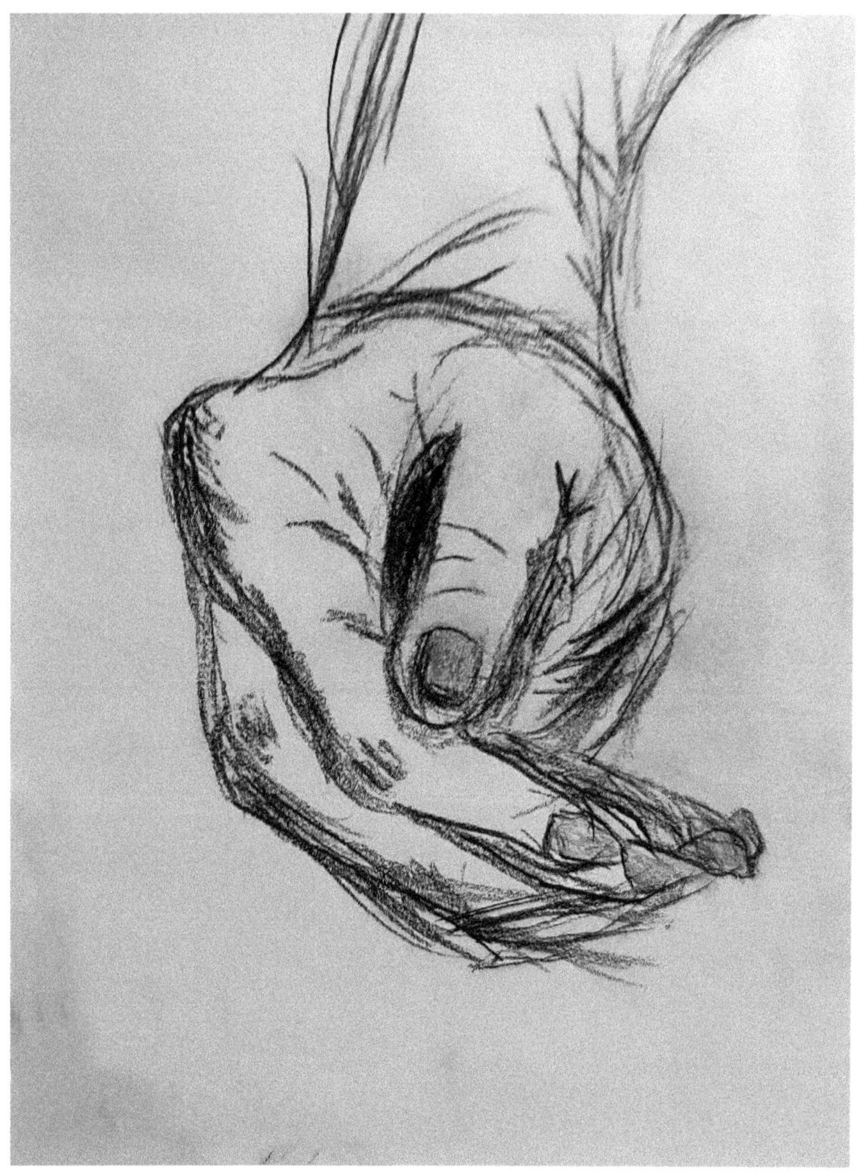

Adjustment

At this point I'm just used to it

Staring into blank space

Staring at hospital ceilings

Staying safe yet trapped just in case

I'll stay on the bathroom seat

Because I do not wish to fall

So I'll wait those 20 more minutes just in case attempting to move is my downfall

Because I can't risk that

That risks too great

It's like I'm in an arena just learning how to skate

My socks could slip

I can't get them off on my own

I'll just sit on the bathroom seat

And call it a throne

I'm waiting for my aids

My living breathing limbs

I could get by without you until

The last straw gives.

G
ORANGE

Antibiotic

It's back they finally say

After weeks of searching

The smoking gun has been found

All you get now is the notification

The antibiotic is ready to pick up

Aren't you excited?!

Go on get it, and then you can heal!

But I'm never met with excitement when I see that notification.

The doctors didn't even have decency to call .

They found the bug gave you meds

Now its on you again doll

My body curses my name.

I'm sorry love I say, we need to heal.

Though it's harder to absorb my own comforts then my pills

No matter how many times I get put on these pills

It doesn't get easier

Like fire drills

My body knows the routine

But doesn't go easy

It had just made the home

Which now it must flee

Camille Soleil

Hospital

It's nice in hospitals yet scary just the same

It's where us humans experience our worst pains

It's nice because we're looked after

Though scary because it's a changing factor

People are always around

Yet you spend a lot of time alone

And they only see you when they round

You're in their palms yet at their mercy

It's a very strange and different courtesy

You're safe

It's just not home

You don't have your freedom to roam

You can't get up and grab your stuff

You have a red button

And for now that's enough

Camille Soleil

Time out

You can't be alone

You'll come apart if you are

You can't be alone

It'll hurt and it will scar

You can't do it.

It's gotten too much

Hand in your towel with the last bit of courage you can muster up

Lay down girl

You're done

Your body is weak

It's time that at long last with grace you admit defeat

But You hate to lose.

That's whats gotten you this far

But we can't keep this fighting

It'll hurt who we are

But even I can't tell you that...

For its in your DNA

Your body knows the fight

It'll beat the decay

Even as strings and stones shatter away....

You'll still be there standing at the end of the day.

Camille Soleil

Untied

I want your life

Although I really do love mine

I want your life

Though then I wouldn't rhyme

Then I wouldn't paint or draw

although perhaps I might

it wouldn't be the same though

And I'd see the great height

That lies in between each of the lives

I couldn't have achieved where I am without the price

At 7 years old my life taught me fast

To do it all now and save anxiety for last

To grin and bear and laugh and cry

To look at blank ceilings and shout loudly "why?"

But it all taught me well and my tears gave me strength

This strength was in gifts

That I chose to take

In drawing and writing and wisdom in spades

Hell I'm 27 and I don't relate to kids of today

I'm not a fan of my aged people

I didn't learn with them

I learnt from the world, from science and the pen

I learnt from experience

I learnt from distress

I learnt from my life much different then the rest

I didn't grow up with mine

I got interfered at 7

Then again at 9, 10, 11

I couldn't find the course

So I did my best

So now no I'm really not the same as the rest

I want your life

But in all honesty I don't

Because in mine I have something you probably won't

Camille Soleil

People Please

I could feed you the words you long to hear

But they wouldn't be true

I could make you drunk with my lies

But that would only please you

It would hurt me more to live like that

To not be truly seen

To live under the positivity umbrella

Where I could no longer beam

My light doesn't always radiate in sun

Most times it's strongest in the dark

It makes my heart hurt that I can't live the life you want for me

Then in turn I get angry

at myself for being unable to be ok

Because I want that

How I so desperately plead all my ailments would just go away

Even for one day

A day in the sun

Tomorrow

I could be living in tomorrow,

All of the dreams that I could borrow.

I could postpone all my sorrow,

If I was living in tomorrow.

Camille Soleil

Kids

Running by the pool

Blowing bubbles in the wind

Squealing with glee

Nothing else on their mind

When does this end

In human kind?

Our focus and presence in the here and now

Your brain is free it hasn't yet developed routines

If you were running on a track all the lanes could be yours

All possibilities all still in store

You're learning from adults while some adults relearn through you

Healing our past traumas we've been through

All to do it just right, for you

We don't want you to go through what we have gone through

You're a tiny little human

That life's barely touched

Unlike most adults caught in its clutch

Blow your bubbles

I see them from my balcony and they heal my soul

There not just for kids

They make me feel more whole

Souls

Somewhere out there in this world

You draw stars in the sand

And live a whole different life

That I'll never understand

Our paths crossed for a year

We went from strangers to friends

Then your world took you out of mine

And we didn't even pretend

One day you were here

We would explore beach towns

Then the next you were gone

And you didn't make a sound

I had forgotten you too

Life had swallowed me up

So, I didn't know to go look for you

And you didn't speak up

By the time I knew

I looked for you in sorrow

I didn't know the last time we spent would now be in memories I borrow

My name sounded extra sweet when it came from your lips

It sounded like ice cream that had been chocolate dipped

You were a friendship

I may only have once

I tiptoed around it so not to destroy it by my lust

we were friends

I wish I could've kept our energy in a bottle.

But I do wonder what life would be now if I had gone full throttle…

Love Camì

Camille Soleil

Flower

I'm beautiful

I'm smart

I'm a candy coated work of art

I'm a forest with a thousand trees

My roots run deep

Fairies dance on the breeze

My life's like gravel under a cowboot

Or like a bull right out of the shoot

Or like a million fireflies on the darkest night

I'm a delicate little flower

I shift with the slightest of wind

But I'll always stay where I'm planted

Even if I must grow slanted

Don't take me for granted

I could leave you stranded

If you treat me wrong

But I'm loyal as ever when I know your worth

I'm just anxiety underneath it all

It makes me so scared that in front of you I could fall

I'm beautiful

I'm smart

I'm a candy coated work of art

Treat me gently

And I'd be yours

Let's live in a land that soars

Camille Soleil

Papa

You deserve some chocolate fondue.
Drinking two beers with every meal,
And you are now 82 ❤
Your life holds so many memories,
And countless stories to tell.
I love hearing them all,
I love you so much this poem I would yell.
You and me are like two peas,
I treasure my Florida adventures with you:
Including.
Catching triple tail you spot from miles away,
Riding the waves.
Then eating the yummy fish at the end of the day.
Putting me in your pocket when I was little.
Holding me snug and making me giggle.
Dates with you at the Crab shack And Pewter mug.
Ordering two alcoholic drinks we'd then have to chug.
Crossword puzzles you'd leave me in the morning,
While hearing you lightly snoring.
"There she is"
You say as I get up for the day.
"You decided to get up"
I slept in but you've been up since 6,
As you pour my morning tea into my teacup.
Our days were always filled with fun, and started with a bike ride.
Around the neighborhood we would go,
Our bikes we'd pedal beside.
Remember when we saw that boat
That had flipped by the road?
In the trench it fell and we sat on our bikes and watched as it was
towed.
Some days we'd go to Joanne and Roger's house,
Or out to watch the hockey game.

First to eat in the club,
Then to cheer on the Everblades in fame.
Because you're famous I hope you know...,
Look at that award you've won.
You've always been by my side,
You're brightness to the world is shown.
Sitting together on the lanai,
Drinking in the Florida sun.
I smile to myself...
I think we should discuss the situation in Spain.
And pop open some champagne.
Cheers to you at 82,
You are my hero.
I love you ❤

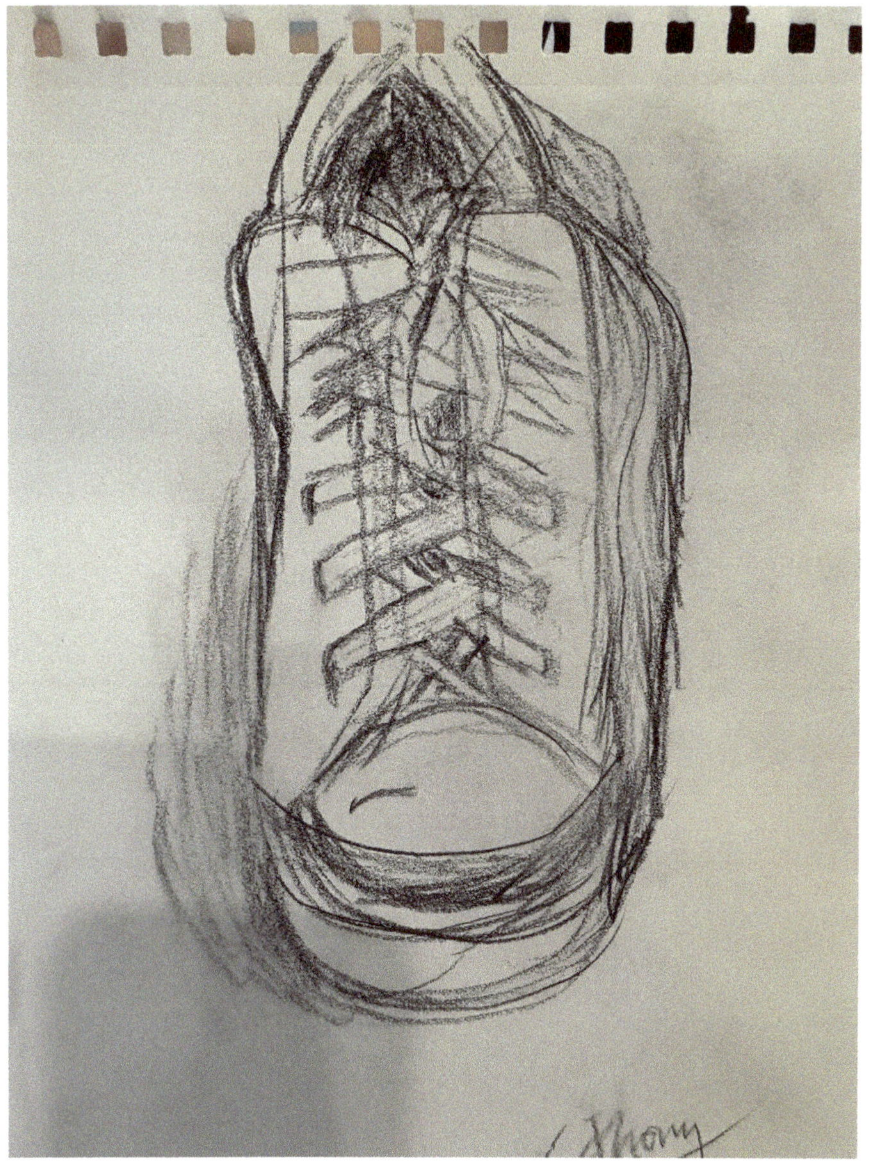

Preserved

I'm so glad I lived life fully.
So now, although still young, I can look back and live in small preserved moments in time.
When I am feeling glum

5 years ago, I lived in Utah
I drove my car as far as I could
I didn't live by a rule book
Though some say I should
I drove in the snow
I walked along ice
I breathed in the cold air between those mountains, and damn, it was nice
I knew what I had when I had it
I just didn't know how much it would change
I didn't know this life I was living
Could see this much range

On Saturday nights during college
I would go to the clubs, drink with my friends.
Get silly and drunk and make out with the guy dancing behind me for the hell of it
We'd wobble home
blast Post-Malone
And giggle at our little lives
"Why'd you do that?"
They'd ask
"How are you so free?"

Camille Soleil

I was astonished at myself, but it just felt like being me
My soul would emerge
It would say, "This is right."
It would grab life by the throat
And say, "We only have tonight."
That girl back then
She could see me now
She wanted to leave me her joys
She wanted to make them say wow

Life gave her the wrong cards.
She wanted to make you pay
My soul said to this life
"I am strong today."

My soul never stopped saying that.
That's how I jumped outta that plane
That's how I danced in Italy
It's how I drank my champagne

It's what made my confidence build
To extraordinary heights
When life said, "you're too weak."
My soul just ignites.

When I'm depressed and down
I get very angry
My body coverts that to energy
And uses that to fuel me

Back in college
I didn't need anger as fuel
Energy came from my friends, rum and cokes, or something more
beautiful

On mornings on my campus
I'd go down to a grassy clearing
Lay out my towel as my thoughts were disappearing
Do a headstand because I could do that
Feel graceful with my feet in the air
Feeling the safety solely from my yoga mat

I walked on my own two feet
Independently although clumsy
Occasionally losing my shoe on the way back from the bars
Just another regular life absurdity

65

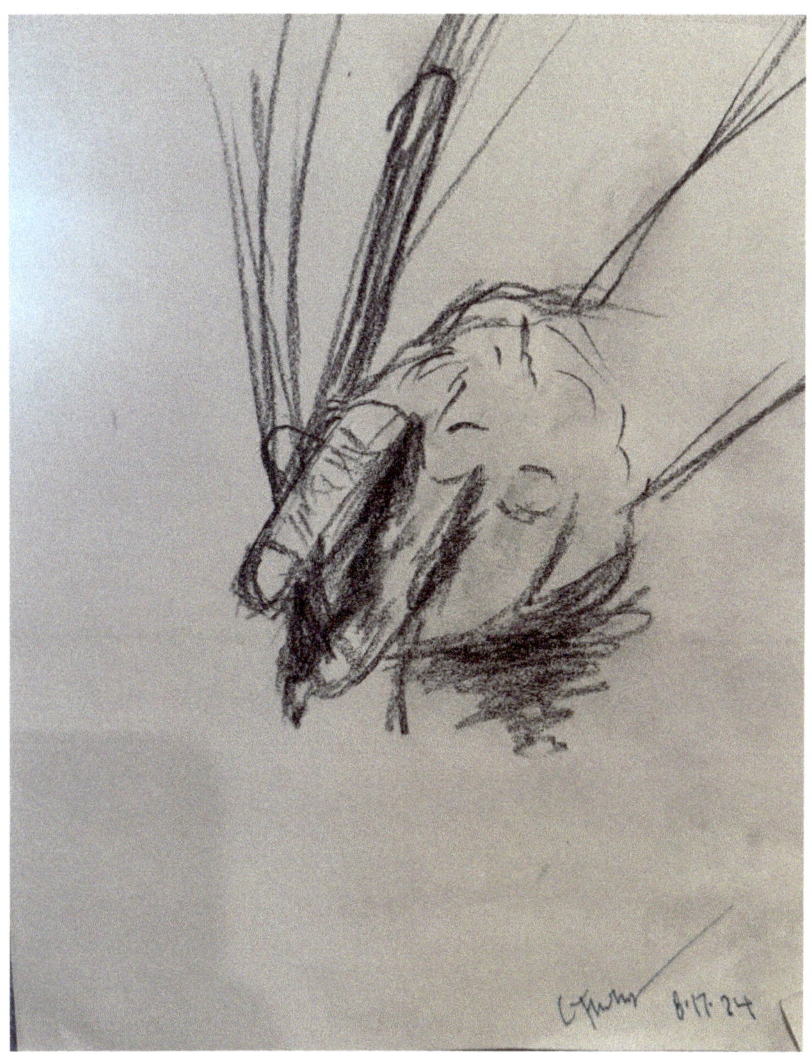

Hope

I'm hoping for good,

Amidst all the bad.

Silver linings I draw on the clouds.

I can't, and I won't let my state become something that hope overcrowds.

Hope is so pure.

Hope is the gas.

It's how I keep myself going.

Though I've learned hope can cause pain,

So, sometimes, I refrain to let others see my hope growing.

For hope can become so beautiful,

The larger it builds.

Each flower I lay in its hands.

Placing each flower makes my hope gain its power,

And I plead that my hope can outlive:

The pain we must go through,

The false positives,

The cycle of routines repeating.

When all can seem lost,

I look for my hope,

To see that it's heart is still beating.

My hope, though, can get sad,

When it sees it couldn't fulfill all of its promises...

Though

Love is what fills the tree and is what is sustaining the flowers,

Love is a strong force that can rebirth some of my dead flowers.

So maybe I don't need to shelter my hope,

In fear, the petals may blow away...

Hope is the one thing that will keep me coming back,

For it still has something to say.

All the pieces

The hunts done

You found it

You found out why you hurt and experience the world like you do.

All the pieces you've been gathering

Like a bear storing food for winter

All the pieces

The goose chase you've been on

You've gathered a lot of them

Look at them all

They look nicer that way

The hardest question to ask and get the answer we want is in that one simple word....why?

For it's not one simple thing wrapped in a bow for you to find

It's not that one Easter egg you're really after because it has the money

No love look down at the basket you're holding from your hunt

It's all of them

Together

Overlapping

Crossfaded

Melted together

Reeces

M&m's

The chocolate bunny

Open them up

Camille Soleil

Examine them all

The deliciousness and the insight in them

That chocolate hiding the peanut butter

*The different colored candy coating revealing the same chocolate
underneath*

The magical chocolate bunny who has nothing inside to find

Sometimes the clues don't help as much as we thought

At times things won't make sense

You'll look fine but be hurt

Babe you're unique

There's nothing else like you

You're all the pieces

Grace

I've been living most of my life stuck in one way

Fight or flight just trying to survive nothing makes it go away

This life is hard what can you do

Something's don't go like they should

But hey....

What can you do but breathe

Give yourself grace they say

You are so strong

Give yourself space they say

From where you went wrong

Then they fight you about how you live your life

And they said to do all these things

I'm just trying to see what each day brings

~Stay close to
people who feel like
Sunshine ~